Retire Successfully

by Following Shortcuts
and Avoiding Hazards

By Craig A. Anderson

Overflowing
resources

Overflowing Resources Publishing Company
2620 S. Cleveland, Suite 205, St. Joseph, MI 49085

ISBN: 978-1-950012-04-6
United States of America

Overflowing Resources Publishing Company is a division of Family Focused Financial. www.famfocfinancial.com | info@famfocfinancial.com

Cover design by Jennifer Cummings, using AI-generated landscape June 10, 2025.

Retire Successfully / Craig A. Anderson—1st ed.

Table of Contents

Copyright Page 2
Credits 4
Introduction 5
The Visit 6
Income, part one 8
Income, part two 18
Income, part three 23
Investment 28
Tax 37
Legacy, part one 47
Legacy, part two 50
Legal 53
Risk 58
Health 63
Legacy, part three 66
Legacy, part four 74
Epilogue 78
Index of Shortcuts and Hazards 80
7 Key Areas for a Successful Retirement 81
Generation Series 82
Connect with the Author 83
About Family Focused Financial 83

Credits

Thank you, editing team, for your patience, observations, and insights while you combed through the manuscript of *Retire Successfully*.

Annabelle West

Linda Diltz

Jenny Cummings

Introduction

So many times, we learn something new and think, "I sure do wish I would have known this 10, 20, or 30 years ago." It's sad when we estimate how much further we might be by now if only we had learned these lessons earlier. We may feel like we missed the bus.

Something even more tragic is when we learn lessons, but we don't apply this wisdom to our lives now. We choose not to get on the bus that could take us where we want to go because we will arrive later than desired. But refusing to get on the bus now only delays our progress even more.

Some of the lessons in this story may be new to you. Some may be familiar. The question is, "Are there any lessons that you need to apply to your life right now so you don't miss the bus that is in the station?"

The Visit

Kim and Sofia sat down together in the busy hospital lunchroom. Right behind them, a loud crash suddenly jolted them and silenced the lively, buzzing sound of conversations circling them.

Everyone turned to look at a blushing nurse's aide-in-training as she leaned over to clean up her spilled lunch. Sofia instinctively helped her scoop most of the mess off the floor, and the girl, though thankful, was deeply embarrassed. She deposited the remains from her tray in the nearest trash can and ran out of the room in tears. Sofia and Kim gave each other a "poor girl" look. Everyone else resumed their conversations as if nothing had happened.

Sofia: How was your vacation?

Kim: The weather was good, and it was great to see my grandparents again, but….

Sofia: But what?

Kim: They are both nice people and all, but they haven't managed their money very well, and…they're just broke. I can tell it really weighs on them.

Sofia: Sorry to hear that.

Kim: They would love to travel and give more to charity, but they can't. They say they would like to help us grandkids more, and you can tell they mean it. They just don't have any money left. My grandma jokes that their "savings is bone dry." Whatever comes in each month is all they have to live on.

Sofia: A lot of people live like that.

Kim: You seem to have your financial act together.

Sofia: I don't know about that, but my husband, Roberto, and I are learning as we go.

Kim: So, my grandparents had two kids: my mom and her sister, Sue. The funny thing is, I don't think my Aunt Sue and her husband even make as much as my parents, but they seem to be in great shape financially.

Sofia: Yeah. It's not really about what you make as much as what you do with it.

Kim: Hmm. My parents have always worked hard, but they never taught us kids how to manage money. Where did you learn?

Sofia: Same here. My parents taught us how to work hard, but most of what I've learned about money came from my Uncle Ron and my financial planner.

Kim: I want to retire someday, but I have no idea how to get there.

Sofia: You want to learn?

Kim: I'd love to.

Sofia: I can teach you.

Kim: You would do that?

Sofia: I still have a lot to learn, but I can share what we've done so far and what I wish I had done earlier.

Kim: That would be awesome!

Sofia: I can show you a few hazards and shortcuts we've learned. What if we have lunch like this once a week and talk through some things?

Kim: I would really like that.

Income

part one

The next week, on a warm, sunny day, Sofia and Kim carried their food to one of the outdoor picnic tables where they could talk privately.

Sofia: How was your weekend?

Kim: Great! I keep thinking about our last conversation.

Sofia: And what did you think about it?

Kim: I'm pretty pumped. The last thing you said really stuck in my head.

Sofia: What was that?

Kim: Shortcuts and hazards. What a great word picture!

Sofia: I heard about it from my financial advisor. "If you want to get to retirement *quickly,* you need to know where the shortcuts are. And if you want to get through retirement *safely,* you need to know where the hazards are." She pointed both out to us.

Kim: That's exactly what I want.

Sofia: Okay. I've been trying to think about where to start. I thought of two big picture ideas.

Kim: Okay, I'm listening.

Sofia: I'm a little nervous.

Kim: Why?

Sofia: I don't see myself as much of a teacher.

Kim: Well, I barely got through nursing school because I'm not much of a student.

They both laughed.

Kim: I love to learn, but I'm more hands-on-practical, if you know what I mean, not very text-booky.

Sofia: That actually puts me at ease because I just did what I was told, and it seems to be working. I don't know if I can explain it very well.

Kim: Give it a shot.

Sofia: Alright, the first thing I wanted to share with you is that you can retire as soon as you can replace your income.

Kim: Yeah. At what age?

Sofia: It doesn't matter how old you are. It only matters if you can replace your income.

Kim: Well, I've always thought you had to work until you were somewhere between 60 and 70. Are you saying if you can replace your income earlier than that, you can retire earlier?

Sofia: Exactly.

Kim: Okay, you have already blown my mind.

Sofia: That easily?

Kim: Wow, replace your income. It's so simple and obvious once you say it, but I've never thought of it that way before.

Shortcut

Build up ways to replace your income

Sofia: The goal isn't to make it to a certain age; it's to build up ways to replace your income. If I had understood this concept sooner, I would probably be retired by now.

Kim: Whoa. Seriously?

Sofia: Yeah, seriously!

Kim: But you're only in your 40s.

Sofia: Thank you. I'm 51.

Kim: So, how can a person replace their income by the time they're 50?

Sofia: That's the second big picture. You need to understand four strategic levers and how they affect one another.

Kim, *pulling out a notebook and pen:* Okay, what are they?

Sofia, *teasing:* You said you weren't a very good student.

Kim, *smiling:* This sounds practical. I need to write it down.

Sofia: The first strategic lever is income itself.

Kim: What do you mean by lever?

Sofia: Levers are tools that move things, right?

Kim: Yes.

Income as Lever #1

Sofia: Well, your income is the first tool that moves you closer to retirement. If you aren't making fast enough progress financially, you can increase your income by getting a raise, a better job, or another job, etc.

Kim: Makes sense. But what difference does it make? Every time I get a raise, I just spend it.

Sofia: That's lever number two.

Spending as Lever #2

Kim: What do you mean?

Sofia: What happens if you don't spend everything you make?

Kim, *laughing:* I've never had that problem.

Sofia, *smiling:* Seriously, what would happen?

Kim: I guess, theoretically, I'd have some money left over.

Sofia: And what if you did that month after month?

Kim: I'd eventually have a lot of money left over. But I don't see the point of that; it doesn't earn much interest just sitting in the bank, and it's certainly no fun.

Sofia: The point is that if you manage lever number two, spending, then you are on your way to building lever number three, assets.

Appreciating assets as Lever #3

Kim: I've heard that term, but I don't really know what it means.

Sofia: An asset is anything you own that has value, like money, a car, a house, or your 401k here at work.

Kim: That's a lot simpler than I thought it would be.

Sofia: But there are two kinds of assets: *appreciating* assets and *depreciating* assets. That's just a fancy way of saying they are going up or down in value over time.

Kim: Like a car would be a depreciating asset?

Sofia: Exactly. And money is a depreciating asset.

Kim: What?

Sofia: Yeah, money is worth less and less over time. It has less buying power because of inflation, so it takes more dollars to buy the same thing a couple years from now.

Kim: That's pretty obvious.

Sofia: Yes. And a house or a 401k plan would each be appreciating assets because they generally go up in value. Appreciating assets are what you want to build.

Kim: But it takes so long for my 401k to grow.

Sofia: That's true at first. But the compounding effect causes it to grow faster and faster over time.

Kim: What do you mean?

Sofia: Let's say you have $1,000 in your 401k plan and it earns 10 percent interest in one year. How much money do you make?

Kim: $100?

Sofia: Right. Now let's say you keep putting more and more money into that plan over the next 25 years, and it grows, and now you have $1,000,000. If it earns 10 percent, how much is that?

Kim, *thoughtfully:* 10 percent of $1,000,000 would be $100,000. Is that right?

Sofia: Yes. It will probably take you many years to save $100,000, but you can make that much in one year with compounding.

Kim: Whoa! That is crazy cool.

Sofia: That's when investing really starts to be fun.

Kim: I could easily live off $100,000 a year.

Sofia: Now you're getting the idea…or at least part of it. We'll come back to that. The last lever is liabilities, or debt.

Kim, *laughing:* Oh, I understand that one! I have a lot of debt, and it keeps growing. But I didn't realize it was a good thing.

Sofia: It isn't necessarily good. You remember I said there are appreciating and depreciating assets?

Kim: Yeah.

Sofia: When you borrow money for anything, you pay more than the retail price, right?

Kim: Not necessarily. I often buy things on sale.

Sofia: But you pay the purchase price plus interest.

Borrowing money as a negative Lever

Kim: That's true, but here's how I see it: If I buy a new sweater for 30 percent off and my credit card is only charging 20 percent, I figure I'm still saving 10 percent. Right?

Sofia: Let's think about that. What's your highest credit card rate?

Kim: I don't know…maybe 21 or 22 percent. I haven't read the fine print.

Sofia: Do you pay your card balance off every month?

Kim: No way.

Sofia: If it takes you a year to pay off your debt, you're paying at least 21 or 22 percent more than the purchase price for everything you buy that way, right?

Kim: Yes, but if I get it at 30 percent off, I'm still ahead.

Sofia: Maybe. How long does it usually take to pay off a credit card?

Kim: I don't. I always make the minimum payment, but it never really gets paid off.

Sofia: Have you figured out how much you are actually paying in interest?

Kim: As I said, maybe 21 or 22 percent.

Sofia, *with a sad smile:* Probably not. It's possible you're paying more in interest than you are for the items you're buying.

Kim: No way!

Sofia: Are any balances more than eight years old?

Kim: Yeah, probably a few of them.

Sofia: I've got an app on my phone. Let's punch in a purchase for $100, okay?

Kim: Okay.

Sofia: And let's say your interest rate is 21.99 percent.

Kim: Sounds about right.

Sofia: Okay, your minimum payment could be as low as $2.22, but over eight years, you end up paying over $213 for that $100 item and even more if you take longer to pay it off.

Kim: I don't believe that. Show me.

Sofia, *handing the phone over to Kim:* I didn't believe it either the first time I saw it. My uncle showed me a mortgage payment schedule, and I thought it couldn't possibly be true.

Kim: All this time I thought I was saving money because I got good deals.

Borrowing for depreciating assets

Sofia: When you borrow for depreciating assets like clothes, you can easily pay more for something that is going down in value.

Kim: Not exactly getting ahead, huh?

Sofia: But if you borrow for appreciating items, it *might* help you get ahead.

Kim: Why do you say, "might"?

Sofia: Sometimes, it will help you get ahead. Sometimes it won't.

Kim: Oh, like…like…. Can you give me an example?

Sofia: Well…let's say you buy an investment property in a growing area. It might be worth quite a bit more after you fix it up.

Kim: Buy an investment property! That's for rich people.

Sofia: You could be wealthy.

Kim: I'm broke.

Sofia: I will say it again…you could be wealthy.

Kim: You sound so confident. You really mean it, don't you?

Sofia: If you're serious about this, then yes, I do.

Kim: I have a lot of poor people in my family. I make more money than most of them because I'm a nurse, but I'm a long way from being rich.

Sofia: That could change.

Kim: Sofia, you're an honest person. It's just that this is all so new to me; I don't know if I believe it.

Sofia: That's okay.

Kim: You're not offended?

Sofia: Not when you tell me I look younger than I am.

They both laughed.

Sofia: Seriously, when my Uncle Ron started me on this journey over 30 years ago, I had no idea how much progress we would make. And if we had found a good financial advisor sooner, we would have moved even faster. I didn't know what I didn't know.

Kim: That's a good way to describe it—I don't know what I don't know.

Income

part two

The next week was sunny and warm, but "their" picnic table was taken, so they sat at one nearby.

Kim: Sofia, I have a favor.

Sofia: Yeah?

Kim: I told my boyfriend, Rick, about our conversation last week, and he would like to join us. Would that be okay?

Sofia: Sure; it's a great idea.

Kim, *looking at a nearby bush and motioning with her head:* Come on, Rick. It's okay.

She turned back to Sofia, laughing sheepishly. Sofia busted out laughing as Rick walked over from behind the bush and sat down with them.

Kim: Sofia, this is my boyfriend, Rick.

Sofia, *reaching out to shake hands:* Nice to meet you, Rick.

Rick, *shaking Sofia's hand nervously:* Nice to meet you.

Kim: When I told Rick about our conversations, he said I was lucky to find someone like you. No one taught him how money works. That's when I said he should join us, but he thought I should get your permission first.

Rick: Thanks for lettin' me join you.

Sofia: It's fine with me. It could really help you two to be on the same page, financially.

Kim: That's what I was thinking. You know Alice, in radiology?

Sofia: Yeah.

Kim: She is always complaining about how she and Eric view money differently and how much it stresses her out.

Sofia: Exactly…one of the top reasons for divorce…money problems.

Kim: I already explained the four levers to Rick. What's next?

Sofia, *opening her lunch and smiling at a brownie:* I'm not sure how, but I want to explain more about how these levers affect each other and how to optimize each one.

Rick: It's easy to see how they affect each other. If you spend less than you make, you build up assets. And if you spend more than you make, you build up debt.

Sofia: Boom! I guess you just saved us a lot of time.

Kim: Wait, what do you mean?

Rick: You're the one who explained it to me.

Kim: Did I?

Rick: Yeah, remember? Sofia told you if you saved a little bit from each paycheck, you could build up wealth.

Kim, *laughing:* Yeah, I guess so. I just didn't take it very seriously because I never have money left over.

Sofia: You could.

Kim: How can you be so sure? I appreciate you taking the time to explain this stuff to me, but I just don't have any hope that my financial situation will improve much more than it already has. Like I said, I already make more than anyone else in my family.

Rick: It absolutely could, Kim. You spend a lot of money on junk with nothing to show for it.

Kim, *offended:* Wait, what are you talking about?

Rick: For starters, all the fancy coffees you get on the way to work.

Kim: I need to wake up.

Rick: And you said you go down to the vending machine for snacks every day.

Kim: It's none of your business if I snack.

Sofia: Whoa! Whoa! These are mice, not walruses.

Rick: What?

Sofia: Rick, I agree with you about how little things can add up, but first, Kim is going to resent you for telling her how to spend her money.

Kim: No kidding!

Sofia: And secondly, if someone really wants to change their financial situation, they need to start with the walruses, not with the mice.

Rick: What is that supposed to mean?

Sofia: It's a word picture my financial advisor gave Roberto and me. We were trying to evaluate our spending, and we were getting pretty critical of each other, just like…well, let's just say it's very easy to criticize how other people waste money and easy to justify how we waste money ourselves.

Kim: That's right, Mr. Video Game.

Rick: Those are collector items.

Kim: Whatever.

Shortcut

Start with the walruses, not the mice

Sofia, *interrupting:* The picture looks like this. You're in a small boat with a bunch of animals, and water comes in every time the waves rock the boat from side to side. If you don't do something about it, you will all drown. Do you worry about the mice, or do you figure out how to get the walruses out of the boat?

Rick: Well, a walrus will have more impact than a mouse.

Sofia: Exactly.

Kim: So…?

Sofia: When you start going over your expenses, you need to find the walruses and not worry about the mice. Initially, try to find the big things instead of the small things. What's really going to move the needle the most?

Rick: Let me think about that.

Kim: Okay, but why do you need to do this at all?

Sofia: If you want to retire early, you need to build assets, preferably ones that generate income. If you want to build assets, you need to spend less than you make. If you want to spend less than you make, you either need to cut your spending or make more money, or both.

Rick: I'm on it. I can already think of some things that are going away.

Kim: I can't think of anything I want to give up. And I don't want to get a second job.

Sofia: It's not that you *want* to give up those things or that you *want* a second job. It's that you do them temporarily because it'll be worth it someday. And you'll get them back later. It's delayed gratification.

Kim: I'm just not sure it's worth it for me.

Sofia: That's a decision you will need to make.

Rick: Kim, are you bailing out on Sofia's tutoring program?

Kim: To be honest, if it means I need to start cutting all the fun things out of life, then I'm not really sure I'm up for that.

Sofia: That's okay. Let's pause. If you want to start back up, just let me know, alright?

Kim, *looking at Rick meaningfully:* Thanks Sofia. I appreciate that *you* aren't putting pressure on me to change.

Rick, *anxiously:* Um, would you keep teaching me?

Sofia, *pausing, then turning to Kim:* Kim, what would you think of that?

Kim: Fine with me. I'm just not sure I'm ready to change everything right now. I like things the way they are and it's comfortable.

Sofia: Okay, Rick. We can keep talking.

Rick: Thanks.

Income

part three

Sofia, *joining Rick at the same table as the week before:* How's Kim doing?

Rick: We're in a rough spot. You may have noticed I'm an all-in kind of guy.

Sofia, *chuckling:* Kinda did notice that.

Rick: I'm getting into this money thing big-time. Every time I bring it up, Kim gets defensive. So, it's starting to pull us apart. I was ready to propose to her, but the way things are going, I'm not sure it's even going to work out for us.

Sofia: I'm sorry to hear that. Do you want to stop?

Rick: No. I'm just seeing a stubborn side of Kim I never saw before, and to be honest, kind of selfish, too. Don't get me wrong, Kim has a lot of good qualities, and I think she's beautiful, but we just seem to be growing apart.

Sofia: Sorry.

Rick: It's all good. We both need to grow up some more. If it's meant to be, it'll work out. If not, it won't.

Sofia: Wow, you seem pretty relaxed about it.

Rick: It is what it is. We both have some growing to do. I have my issues, too. It's not all her. Whether it works out with Kim or not, I need to get my financial act together.

Sofia: Alright then.

Rick: Besides, with Kim, most new ideas that aren't hers are bad ideas, but she often comes around after she's had time to think about them for a while.

Sofia: Okay. Let's talk some more about how these levers impact us long term.

Rick, *pulling out his cell phone and hitting record:* I'm ready.

Sofia: What do you think is the most important lever?

Rick: That's easy. Assets. The sooner you build up a large pile of cash, the sooner you can start living off it.

Sofia: Nope.

Rick: Why not?

Sofia: A few reasons. First, money is a depreciating asset. It becomes worth less and less over time. Inflation could eat up your nest egg because you need more and more to buy things in retirement.

Rick: Didn't think of that.

Sofia: Second, there's an even more powerful lever than assets.

Rick: Income?

Sofia: Nope. It's expenses.

Rick: I don't get it. Why are expenses powerful?

Sofia: Well, how much do you need to live on?

Rick: I don't know.

Sofia: Let's say you have $1,000,000 and no debt, and you need $50,000 a year to cover expenses. You need to earn 5 percent of your money to cover your income.

Rick: Can you explain that?

Sofia: Sure. What is 5 percent of $1,000,000?

Rick: Uh, $50,000?

Sofia: Right. If you earn $50,000 and spend $50,000, you still have $1 million.

Rick: Got it.

Sofia: Now what if you need $100,000 a year to live on?

Rick, *calculating quickly in his head:* You need to earn 10 percent?

Sofia: That's right. Every year.

Rick: Well, doesn't the market average about 10 percent a year?

Sofia: Probably, over time. But does it make that much every single year?

Rick: No. Why does that matter as long as it averages out?

Sequence of return risk

Sofia: It doesn't matter if you are adding to your money or just letting it grow. But once you retire and start pulling money out, everything changes.

Rick: What do you mean?

Sofia, *pulling out her phone and punching numbers into the calculator:* Let's say the market drops 20 percent in the first year of retirement. Is that possible?

Rick: Oh, yeah.

Sofia: So, if your $1,000,000 drops to $800,000, *and* you pull out $100,000 to live on. How much do you have?

Rick: Ouch. $700,000.

Sofia, *still calculating:* You need to make 14.28 percent every year from now on. And that won't bring your money back to a million. And you won't ever get a cost-of-living raise.

Rick: Yikes. That's not a very good plan, is it?

Sofia: Not exactly. I'll talk more about how to set up your investments next time, so this won't be so much of a problem. But, let me ask you this: What if you cut your spending by 20 percent instead of doubling it? Now, because you cut your spending by 20 percent you can live off $40,000 instead of $50,000 per year. And let's say that allows you to save 20 percent more, so you end up with $1,200,000 instead of $1,000,000 over the same time frame.

Rick, *pausing the recorder and calculating on his phone:* $40,000 from $1,200,000…you would only need…3 percent. That seems more doable.

Sofia: Right. That is why getting rid of debt and getting control of spending are so important for a successful retirement. These two are the levers that pull us backward. And income and assets are the two levers that push us forward.

Rick: Okay, increase income and assets, and reduce spending and debts?

Sofia: You got it. If you do all four of those things at the same time, you just put rocket fuel in your race car and found a huge shortcut to retirement.

Rick: I think we just stepped over a line from intriguing to life-altering.

Sofia smiled at the déjà vu.

Investment

Sofia, *at a new table and waving her hand in the air:* Rick, I'm over here.

Rick, *plopping his food down and plunging into the conversation:* Hey Sofia, I've been thinking. Doesn't Social Security provide income in retirement?

Sofia: Yeah.

Rick: Well, doesn't that mean you need to take less out of your investments?

Sofia: Yeah. But that doesn't start until somewhere between the ages of 62 and 70.

Rick: Oh.

Sofia: If you retire early, or delay Social Security benefits, you need to cover your expenses entirely until then. And once you start Social Security, you will still need more income over time because of inflation.

Rick: Okay. You said there was a better investment plan than just pulling 10 percent out of your 401k every year.

Paths to become a millionaire

Sofia: Yeah. That is what I wish I'd known when I was younger. My financial advisor said she sees people become millionaires in three different ways, or a combination of the three.

Rick, *turning on his recorder app:* And they are?

Sofia: We talked about one of them last time. You set aside money from each paycheck, and it compounds over time in the stock market.

Rick: Since last week, I went and looked at my 401k more closely and found out my company matches whatever I put in, up to 6 percent.

Sofia: That's free money.

Rick: And some people don't even put anything in there!

Sofia: Yup. They're missing out.

Rick: What else?

Sofia: The second way to obtain wealth is real estate, which is what my uncle taught me a little about, and the third way is building a business.

Rick: Which one do you wish you had known about sooner?

Sofia: All three.

Rick: Like…would you have done all three?

Sofia: Like…I am doing all three now.

Rick: That sounds overwhelming.

Sofia: Not really. How much time does it take to set money aside in your 401k?

Rick: It doesn't; it happens automatically.

Sofia: And the company matches some of it, so that's a no-brainer.

Rick: Yep, but starting a business?

Sofia: Did you ever mow your lawn at home?

Rick: Still do.

Sofia: What about shoveling snow off your driveway?

Rick: Yes. Those are ways I help my folks, since they aren't charging me rent.

Sofia: If you did that for your neighbors it could become a business.

Rick: How does that get you a million dollars?

Sofia: It doesn't, but did Kim tell you about compounding?

Rick: Yeah, that's one of the things that caught my attention.

Sofia: My uncle taught a neighbor kid how to work. He got a job at a pizza place and eventually he took over three different restaurants.

Rick: Wow!

Sofia: The more skills we learn in running a business, the more likely we are to be able to run a business and the more businesses we can grow. I see this as a form of compounding.

Rick: But mowing lawns doesn't have any compounding potential.

Sofia: What if you hire and teach other kids to mow lawns, and you just get the jobs and collect the money?

Rick: Now that sounds even better.

Sofia: I'm not necessarily recommending you mow lawns. I'm just saying you can grow almost any kind of business.

Rick: Yeah, I don't like that kind of work. So, what else could I do?

Sofia: Kim mentioned video games.

Rick, *brightening up:* Yeah?

Sofia: Ever think about starting a business selling those?

Rick: I don't really want to get rid of those.

Sofia: None of them?

Rick: Well, not certain ones.

Sofia: Does your neighborhood ever have garage sales?

Rick: A couple of big ones every summer.

Sofia: Could you find more video games?

Rick: That's how I got some of the best ones, and crazy cheap!

Sofia: What if you go around to different neighborhoods and find bargains and then sell them online?

Rick: Ooohhhh, that would be a blast!

Sofia: Better than mowing lawns?

Rick: Definitely.

Sofia: You just started a business.

Rick: But how could a business like that compound?

Sofia: You can only get around to so many garage sales, right?

Rick: That's for sure.

Sofia: What if you have other people keeping their eyes open for you?

Rick: Well, I could cover a lot more ground that way, but they wouldn't necessarily know the good video games from the junk.

Sofia: Have them send you a picture, and then you decide for them.

Rick: I like that.

Sofia: You could pay them a finder's fee for anything that is worthwhile, and a bonus for "jackpot" items that are worth a lot of money. Over time, you could teach them the difference.

Rick, *excitedly:* That could totally work. I can think of two friends that would probably be happy to do this for me.

Sofia: If your business grows enough, you start a little kiosk in the mall. If it keeps growing, you move to a storefront. If it keeps growing, you use some of the income to buy a commercial building. You use part of the building for your business and rent part of it out to other tenants. Now you own a business, and you are buying real estate.

Rick: That's genius. But could it grow that much?

Sofia: Maybe. You may have to branch out into other collectibles: trading cards, movies, commemorative coins, comic books, things like that.

Rick, *his excitement growing even more:* That would be a blast!

Sofia: One advantage of having local customers is that you won't have to deal with shipping and postage.

Rick: Ugh!

Sofia: And you build a loyal base of repeat customers.

Rick: I can think of five or six people that would be regular customers right away.

Sofia: Now, if you ever want to semi-retire, teach and pay someone to manage the business, and you collect the profits. Plus, you are getting rent from the building. Once you're fifty-nine and a half, you can also pull some money out of your 401k penalty-free, or you can leave it alone and let it grow longer.

Rick: I could see myself doing something like this for a long time. It wouldn't even be like work.

Sofia: Well, it is a lot of work, but this is the general idea! And if you stop enjoying it, you sell the business and transfer the money into other assets.

Rick: Like what?

Semi-retiring and/or renting out space

Sofia: Maybe you could buy a larger commercial building full of tenants. And you could buy some mutual funds that will keep growing. And maybe you could buy an annuity that will send you a paycheck every month for the rest of your life. And maybe you could start bargain shopping for larger items and reselling them. That way, you aren't putting all your eggs in one basket.

Rick: I understood everything you just said, except the annuity. What's that?

Sofia: It's the opposite of a mortgage.

Rick: Okay?

Sofia: With a mortgage, you borrow X amount of money from the bank and then you pay it back over time, plus interest. Right?

Rick, *still puzzled:* Yeah….

Sofia: Well, with an annuity, the insurance company borrows X amount of money from you and pays you back, over time, plus interest.

Rick: Why not just put it in the bank and draw interest? Wouldn't that be simpler?

Sofia: Yes, but there are a few big differences.

Rick: What are they?

Sofia: With the bank, interest rates change over time, so there's no guarantee how much you will make over the long term.

Rick: Right, but….

Get an annuity

Sofia: The insurance company will tell you up front how much they will pay you every month. Some annuities have payments that increase over time, to help you keep up with inflation. Here's the biggest difference. If you use all the money in the annuity because you live too long, they will keep paying you for the rest of your life, guaranteed. The bank is *not* going to do that!

Rick, *impressed:* Wow, that makes things a lot more predictable.

Sofia: Absolutely. But I would only do this with one bucket of money. I would make sure to use several different buckets as well.

Rick: I was gonna ask you that. Why so many options?

Sofia: One of the best ways to reduce risk is to diversify your portfolio. That is what they mean when they say, "Don't put all your eggs in one basket."

Rick: Okay, but why is that so important?

Don't put all your eggs in one basket

Sofia: You never know which investments are going to do well and which ones will do poorly during a certain season of time. The stock market has done well over many years, but not every year. The real estate market does well over time, but what if you lose your biggest tenant?

Rick: Good point.

Sofia: Business is a great way to build wealth, but what if it slows down during a recession? If you depend on only one of these options, you are more vulnerable. If you put all your money in one bucket and it doesn't do well for a few years, that could really set you back. But if you have all of them, you are spreading out your risk *and* compounding your wealth.

Rick: That makes total sense, but if I can get a guaranteed paycheck from an annuity for the rest of my life, why not just put everything in there? It won't take any work at all.

Sofia: Good question. For one thing, you will probably want to keep growing your assets instead of depleting them. For example, you will need extra money, on top of your regular paycheck, for special projects.

Rick: Like what?

Sofia: Like replacing a roof or purchasing a vehicle or taking a big trip.

Rick: I got it.

Sofia: And you may want to leave money to your kids, or a charity, or both.

Rick: You're probably right. I hope to have kids, and it would be nice to leave them something.

Sofia: Lastly, I think God hardwired us to "be fruitful and multiply."

Rick: And that means…?

Sofia: I think it means we are made to build a family and to keep growing our assets. It's not only satisfying to see things grow, but the more we have the more we can help other people.

Rick: That's a cool way to look at it.

Sofia: There's a lot more we could talk about regarding investments, but that's probably enough for now.

Rick: Thanks, Sofia.

Sofia: You're welcome.

Rick: No, I really mean it. This is like…I can already tell it's changing the financial trajectory of my life.

Sofia: I'm glad to hear that. It's worth sharing these things with you.

Tax

Sofia: Hi Rick!

Rick held up his hand as if to wave, but neither his hand nor his face reflected his usual excitement. No sooner did he sit down did it start to rain, so they went inside the lunchroom to find a table.

Sofia: Are you okay?

Rick: Not really. Kim broke up with me.

Sofia: Sorry to hear that.

Rick: It was probably for the best. We really were going in two different directions.

Sofia: Differences can really tear a relationship apart.

Rick: I've seen it coming the last few weeks and thought I could just let go and move on.

Sofia: Yeah?

Rick: I didn't realize how much I cared for her.

Sofia: I'm *really* sorry.

Rick, *frustrated:* Not only that, but I just filed my tax return. That was depressing!

Sofia, *smiling sadly:* You're not having a very good week.

Rick: Ya' think? Well, at least I'm done with taxes.

Sofia: Filling out your return?

Rick: No, paying them.

Sofia, *jokingly:* Actually, you're just getting started.

Rick: What do you mean?

Sofia: You said you are contributing to your 401k?

Rick: Yeah. It's the only part of my income that gets any break at all.

The ticking tax bomb

Sofia: Well, the IRS is *patiently* waiting for their share. You don't really get a break, just a delay.

Rick, *shocked:* What?!

Sofia: All that money you're setting aside.

Rick: Yeah?

Sofia: When you retire, all the money you take out of your 401k is taxable. It's not all yours.

Rick: Whoa.

Sofia: And even in retirement you can owe taxes on some of your Social Security income.

Rick: Hmm. Tax Freedom Day!

Sofia: What's that?

Rick: My business math teacher told us about it. He said we work so many days each year for the government. Tax Freedom Day is the first day each year we start working for ourselves.

Sofia: I've never heard of that.

Rick: Yeah, we work for the government until mid-April sometime. That represents how much we pay in taxes every year. What we make after that represents how much of our income is really ours.

Sofia: I believe it.

Rick: So, why work so hard to put money aside if it's just going to go to the government?

Sofia: There are things you can do to reduce the long-term tax load on yourself.

Rick: Like what?

Sofia: Do you have a Roth option in your 401k?

Rick: Yeah, but my understanding is that it still gets taxed.

Sofia: Right. When you put it in, but not when you take it out. So, put some into your regular pre-tax 401k, where you get a tax break now, and put some into Roth, where you don't.

Rick: Why would I do that?

Sofia: Some companies match the pre-tax amount. That's free money.

Rick: Ours does that.

Sofia: Plus, you get a tax break on those contributions now.

Rick: So, why not put everything in the pre-tax part?

Sofia: Well, you must pay taxes on it when you take it out.

Rick: Oh, that's right.

Sofia: Now, because of the standard deduction, you might not have to pay any, or very much, in taxes when you take out your 401k money in retirement, but tax rules change.

Rick: Alright.

Sofia: Rick, do you remember how the money you contribute compounds over time?

Rick: Yeah. When Kim explained it to me that's how she caught my attention.

Sofia: Well, let's call your contributions the "seed" and the compounding over time the "harvest."

Rick: Alright. I get that.

Pay taxes on the seed instead of the harvest

Sofia: Would you rather pay taxes on the seed or the harvest?

Rick, *slowly:* Ooohhh. I'd rather pay taxes on the seed.

Sofia: There you go. Put most of your retirement contributions into the Roth portion.

Rick: What's the point of that?

Sofia: Well, once it's in a Roth IRA, you never have to pay taxes on it again.

Rick: So what? You already did.

Sofia: On the seed, but not the harvest.

Rick: You mean you don't have to pay taxes on *any* of the growth?

Sofia: Nope. The longer you leave it alone and the more it grows the better.

Rick: Wow, that's cool.

Sofia: Now, there are some other strategies to help reduce the taxes on your pre-tax money.

Rick: Like what?

HSAs and QCDs

Sofia: Like HSAs and QCDs.

Rick: What are those?

Sofia: If you have a high-deductible health plan that allows you to make Health Saving Allowance contributions, those are pre-tax. But when you spend the money on qualified medical expenses, it's not taxable income…tax free going in, tax free coming out!

Rick: I like that.

Sofia: And when you get to the age of 75, you will *have* to start taking money out of your pre-tax 401k (traditional IRA). It's called a Required Minimum Distribution. That's when you pay taxes on the harvest.

Rick: Is that an RMD?

Sofia, *looking impressed:* It is, actually.

Rick: I thought that it started at age 70 ½.

Sofia: It used to. But now it's age 73, or for people born after 1960, it's 75. That's us.

Rick: Nice. But you said QCD.

Sofia: Yes. A Qualified Charitable Distribution is when you send your RMD directly to a charity.

Rick: Oh.

Sofia: You satisfy your RMD and help charity at the same time. Again, tax-free on the way in and on the way out. The only one left out in the cold is the IRS.

Rick: Oh, I like that.

Sofia, *sarcastically:* You're kind of heartless.

Rick, *smiling:* Totally.

Sofia: Back to the subject. If you're going to give charitable gifts anyway, why not avoid taxes at the same time?

Rick: Love it.

Sofia: And you can do Roth conversions.

Shortcut

Roth conversions

Rick: I've heard of those. What are they?

Sofia: It's where you pay the taxes on part of your 401k or Traditional IRA now and turn it into a Roth IRA.

Rick: So, you're paying taxes on the seed instead of the harvest.

Sofia: Exactly.

Rick: How soon should you do that?

Sofia: How much harvest do you want to pay taxes on?

Rick: None, but then I lose the tax deduction for setting aside pre-tax money, don't I?

Sofia: Yes, I would work with a financial planner or accountant to figure out how much to convert each year, if that's even an option.

Rick: What's the point of that?

Sofia: It's still the seed and harvest principle. You're just converting some of the harvest. Not as good as starting sooner, but better than waiting another 20 or 30 years. That's when the compounding really takes off.

Rick: Makes sense.

Sofia: Here's one more idea I wish I had known about sooner. Life insurance.

Life insurance

Rick: Doesn't sound very exciting. I die, and someone else gets the money.

Sofia: Yes, that's one way to use life insurance.

Rick: I thought that was the only way to use it.

Sofia: Life insurance has a couple of cool features built in. For starters, you can pull income out of a life insurance policy tax-free, especially if you want to retire early.

Rick: I'm interested in that, but can't you just use Roth IRA money?

Sofia: Yes, after you turn 59 ½, but if you take earnings out before that, they are taxed and penalized.

Rick: Whoa…I guess not.

Sofia: So, if you set up an insurance policy early enough, by the time you are in your early 50s, you can start taking income out tax-free.

Rick: Okay. I like that idea.

Sofia: And even if you don't need it for income, many policies allow you to pull money out to help pay for long-term care expenses.

Rick: I don't think that'll ever be an issue for me.

Sofia: Of course not, you're a guy and you're in your 20s. But think about your grandparents.

Rick: Yeah?

Sofia: That's you someday.

Rick: Oh. You're right. I guess I always think of myself at my current age.

Sofia: Naturally. Anyway, it would be great to have the insurance company help with these expenses instead of spending down your life savings. Right?

Rick: Totally. I just don't want to worry about that until I get closer to needing it.

Sofia: Then it might be too late.

Rick: What do you mean?

Sofia: You need to be insurable to get an insurance policy set up.

Rick: Meaning?

Sofia: Meaning if you wait until you need it, it'll be too late. They won't sell you insurance because of the risk.

Rick: Oh, that stinks.

Sofia: Besides, you need time for your payments to compound. You can't take money out of a policy that has no cash value built up.

Rick: Right.

Sofia: Make sense?

Rick, *sarcastically*: Yep. Thanks, Sofia. I went from breaking up with my girlfriend and paying taxes to needing long-term care and dying. You really know how to cheer a guy up.

Sofia: Sorry, not very good timing. Maybe we should've skipped talking today.

Rick: I'm just messin' with you. My soccer coach used to say, "Those who *place* the ball win, those who *chase* the ball lose."

Sofia: That was good advice.

Rick: You're basically saying the same thing. Think ahead.

Sofia: Hmm. I guess you're right.

Sofia: Rick, I'm praying for you and Kim.

Rick: Thanks. We both need it.

Legacy

part one

Kim, *approaching Rick and Sofia:* Hi guys. Mind if I join you?

Sofia, *pleasantly surprised:* Come on over.

Rick, *in a curious and friendly tone:* Hey Kim. What brings you back?

Kim: I just got back from my grandparents again. I was talking to Papa alone and found out Nana is the reason why they don't have any money. He wasn't angry, just sad, but I could tell things could have been a lot different if they could have agreed on it.

Sofia: How so?

Kim: He wanted to save money for trips so they could travel, but Nana spent every paycheck before the next one came in. He wanted to help us grandkids with college, but…well, same thing. He had dreams of what they would do in retirement but now they are just in survival mode.

Rick: Wow, that is sad.

Kim: Then he turned to me and said pretty much the same thing you guys were saying, but somehow, he got through to me. I'm like Nana in a lot of ways, and I've always looked up to her, but I realized she has been selfish and shortsighted. Does that sound like anyone else you know?

She started laughing after an awkward moment, which invited Rick and Sofia to join in.

Kim: I started thinking about my lifestyle and how I'm going to end up just like Nana and Papa…. And that is not really where I want to be. *(With a heavy sigh)* It's time to change some bad habits.

Rick: That's really cool, Kim.

Sofia: Thanks for telling us that.

Kim, *looking down:* My mind has been closed to new ideas, but I usually come around when I recognize they're good ones.

Rick winked at Sofia.

Sofia: Well, your timing is interesting because today we were going to talk about Legacy Living.

Kim: What does that mean?

Sofia: Imagine you're at a funeral.

Rick: Sofia has a great way of picking you up, doesn't she?

They all laugh.

Kim: Whose funeral?

Sofia: Yours.

Rick: Like I said.

Sofia: What do you hope people will say about you?

Rick: Seriously, that is a great question.

Kim: I hope people say how loving and generous I was…that I really cared for people.

Rick: I agree.

Sofia: Is that what they would say if your funeral was next week?

Rick: Whoa, let's not rush things.

Sofia: What do you think they would say?

Kim: Wow, I'm a lot like Nana. Most of my money and time are about what will make *me* happy. I don't think very many people would actually say those things about me right now.

Rick: Like, literally no one would say that about me.

Sofia: Let's say you're standing before God. What do you want him to say about you?

Rick: Man, you're going deep today.

Kim: I've never thought about that before.

Rick: Neither have I.

Sofia: Here's the thing. Legacy living is simple, but not easy. Just live so people will say the things you would want them to say at your funeral, and so God will say, "Welcome home, well done."

Rick, *sarcastically:* Oh, that's all.

Sofia:. I didn't say it was easy, just simple.

Kim: So, how do you get people to say those things?

Sofia: That's the question: How do you?

Rick: Not giving us the answer this time?

Kim: She wants to make us think. Right?

Sofia pulled out a brownie and smiled at it.

Legacy

part two

The next week they reconvened inside the lunchroom because outside it was unusually chilly and windy. Kim was the first one to arrive, and she waved the other two over to her table.

Rick: Sofia, you have a way of dropping thought-bombs.

Sofia, *smiling:* Is that good or bad?

Kim: I went through my normal week, but I can't get your question out of my head.

Rick: Yeah, that's what I'm talking about.

Sofia: So, what have you come up with?

Rick, *to Kim:* You first.

Kim: I want to be generous, but I never seem to have enough money. So, I started thinking about your walrus picture.

Sofia: Any ideas?

Kim: Yes. I don't like it, but I know what I need to do.

Rick: What's that?

Kim: My cousin keeps asking if she can buy my car. Since I live at home, it's the biggest expense I have, and she's willing to pay me what I still owe on the car loan.

Rick: Whoa, you love that car!

Kim: I know, but it's keeping me from doing so many other things.

Sofia: How so?

Kim: My parents have an extra car they would let me drive. If I didn't have car payments, it would free up hundreds of dollars a month.

Sofia: Wow, that's a great opportunity.

Kim: Between you guys and Papa, you've really got me thinking.

Sofia: About what?

Kim: I think I've been more concerned about making an *impression* on other people than making an *impact* on them. If I want to be remembered as a generous person, then I need to become a generous person.

Rick: That's really good, Kim. I've been thinking along the same lines.

Sofia, *turning to Rick:* What have you come up with?

Rick: I already drive a clunker so there's not much play there. I'm realizing how much money I blow on video games, movies, and eating out. I started saving a little after I joined this, uh, ninja money group of yours, but it was still all about me.

Sofia: I'm not saying you can't do fun things. Part of legacy living is making a bucket list of things you want to have or do and putting target dates on the calendar.

Rick: Okay, that's good to know. But I didn't think about helping other people at all, like zero.

Sofia: Oh.

Rick: There's this neighbor kid that's always bugging me to spend time together.

Sofia: Nice.

Rick: Well, not really. I pretty much just make excuses as to why I'm too busy.

Kim, *sarcastically:* Real nice!

Rick: Right? Well, the other day I overheard my parents talking about how his dad left recently. I didn't know that. When I found out, I was like, "What a goon I've been."

Kim: That's too bad.

Rick: He just needs an older brother to hang out with.

Sofia: That could make a huge difference in his life.

Rick: Yeah. I pretty much know what I need to do. I just need to take the time.

Kim: To do what?

Rick: Like what Sofia's doing for us. I could teach him about how money works, how to use a knife and build a fire, how to play different sports. I don't know, stuff I wish my older brother would have done with me.

Sofia: That sounds like a great idea.

Kim: My aunt has this rare disease, and they need money for the treatment. I could help them if I got rid of my car.

Sofia: You guys are getting it.

Rick: Well, not the God part. I don't get that.

Sofia: Okay, we'll talk about that sometime.

Legal

Kim had to work during their regular meeting time so only Rick was available to meet with Sofia.

Rick, *approaching the picnic table:* Hey Sofia, what're you working on?

Sofia: I'm looking over our estate planning documents.

Rick: You mean like a will?

Sofia: Yeah, a will and other documents too.

Rick: Why are you going over them?

Sofia: We need to update our instructions because our last child is about ready to leave the house. And we are in a totally different financial situation now than when we were first married.

Rick: I see. Well, I don't have to worry about that for a long time.

Sofia: Why is that?

Rick: Because I'm not married, and I don't have kids.

Sofia: So, who is going to pay for your final expenses?

Rick: You mean like a funeral?

Sofia: Yeah, and any leftover bills?

Rick: I don't know. I never thought about that.

Sofia: Most people don't.

Rick: Literally, most people?

Sofia: Yeah, maybe around two-thirds of people die without any estate plan in place.

Rick: What happens then?

Sofia: The state decides what happens to their stuff.

Rick: What if that's not what they wanted?

Sofia: They have the chance to spell out their wishes before they die.

Rick: But, if you die without a will, the state decides what to do with your stuff?

Sofia: Yep.

Rick: Oh, so maybe I don't want to wait until I'm old to take care of this?

Sofia: Anyone over eighteen should think about it.

Rick: Why so young?

Sofia: Let's say you become disabled. Who do you want to represent you medically? Or for business purposes?

Rick: Not very likely, but I see your point.

Sofia: Power of Attorney documents would authorize the person you choose to represent you for each of these. And you need a will or trust for after you die.

Rick: What's the difference between a will and a trust?

Sofia: They can both be used to distribute assets.

Rick: That sounds redundant.

Sofia: If someone has a simple estate and only one child, they might only need a will, or not even that. Let's say a widow lives in a mobile home and owns one car, two bank accounts, three cats, and four thousand knickknacks.

Rick: You just described my Aunt Betsy.

Sofia: Well, that's a pretty simple estate to distribute.

Rick: How so?

Sofia: The mobile home and car are going to be transferred to the child through the secretary of state or the department of motor vehicle office in most states because they are vehicles.

Rick: Okay, did not realize a mobile home was considered a vehicle.

Sofia: And if there are POD (pay on death) designations on the bank accounts, they pass directly to beneficiaries without going through probate.

Rick: So far so good. Who gets the cats?

Sofia: Depends on who wants them.

Rick, *laughing:* No one.

Sofia: Well, maybe someone would.

Rick: Doubt it. Facebook marketplace.

Sofia: And the knickknacks can go to a thrift store unless someone in the family rescues them.

Rick: You're right, that was easy. What if the situation is more complicated?

Sofia: Let's say there is a remarriage with two sets of kids. Or there is property owned in more than one state. Or there is a special-needs child in the family. Or there is a family business, or farm, or cottage at the lake.

Rick: What happens then?

Sofia: The way it's been described to me, these might all require not just a will, but probably a trust.

Rick: Why?

Sofia: A will can usher stuff through probate to the assigned beneficiaries, but it still goes through probate. If anyone wants to contest the will, they can do so during the probate process.

Rick: So what?

Sofia: Well, if they win their argument, the will might not be followed as the deceased person intended.

Rick: Oh.

Sofia: And if they lose, they have still cost the family legal expenses, delays, and probably hard feelings that will never heal.

Rick: Oh. I have a friend who refers to one side of his family as the Hatfields and McCoys because they are still feuding over grandma's stuff from, like, from 15 years ago.

Sofia: I've heard a lot of horror stories like that.

Rick: And it was over, like, $37,000 and a clothes dresser, or something like that.

Sofia: That's where a trust can be helpful.

Rick: What's the difference? Tell me again.

Sofia: A will and trust can both be used as distribution tools to get rid of stuff, but if everything is set up right, things in a trust don't have to go through probate.

Rick: What difference does that make?

Sofia: Then, everything is distributed privately, so there isn't really an opportunity to contest anything, and the family can save some money on court fees.

Rick: Got it. How do you know which one to use, a will or trust?

Sofia: An elder planning attorney can help you set things up to match your situation and what you're trying to accomplish.

Rick: Thanks for explaining all that to me.

Risk

Sofia's phone rang at 1:47 a.m. It yanked her up from a deep sleep.

Sofia: Hullo?

Kim: Sof, I'm so sorry to wake you up. I didn't know who to call. My parents are out of town.

Sofia: That's okay. What's up?

Kim: One of Rick's friends called me. They were in a crash and Rick's in the ER.

Sofia, *suddenly wide awake:* What? Are they okay?

Kim: I'm not sure. They are both being treated, but separately, so Kurt doesn't know for sure how Rick is doing. Kurt was able to call me. He has some cuts and bruises, but they got split up, so he doesn't know what's going on with Rick.

Sofia: Oh, my.

Kim: I'm on my way there…wondering if you could meet me?

Sofia: Of course. I'll come right away.

Within 10 minutes, Kim arrived at the emergency room. While she was waiting in line at the receptionist's desk, Sofia arrived, rushed to Kim's side, and gave her a hug.

Sofia, with her arm over Kim's shoulder: Let's see what we can find out.

The woman at the reception desk confirmed that Rick had been brought to the ER, but she did not have any additional information. They didn't see Kurt, so they wondered if he was still being treated for his own injuries.

Just then, Veronica, a co-worker and fellow nurse Kim and Sofia both knew, slipped a form onto the receptionist's desk. Looking up, she recognized Kim and Sofia.

Veronica: Sofia! Kim! What are you doing here?

Kim: I'm here to see Rick, my...

She trailed off, not knowing how to finish.

Veronica, *understanding:* Oh...meet me at that door over there.

Moments later, Veronica led them down the hall to Rick's room. Sleeping, Rick was hooked up to IVs and his head was bandaged.

Kim, *rushing to his side:* Oh, Rick!

Sofia turned to hug Kim, who started to cry. She just hung on and sobbed.

Kim, *finally pulling away and wiping her face with a tissue:* I didn't know who to call. My parents are gone, and you're one of my closest friends, and I know you pray a lot....

Sofia: Is it okay if we pray right now?

Kim: Yes, please.

Sofia hugged Kim again and spoke softly. She prayed for Rick, for Kim, for the medical staff attending Rick, and for the surgeon.

When she said, "Amen," she started letting Kim go, but Kim hung on.

Finally, Kim let go and sighed.

Kim, *wiping her eyes:* I didn't realize how much I still care for Rick.

Sofia smiled and sighed.

Soon the ER doctor came in and explained that Rick would need surgery. They had many questions, especially from Sofia, who had more years of nursing experience at the hospital. The doctor answered their questions and left.

Kim, *decisively:* We need to go wake Rick's parents up and let them know what's going on. Kurt said someone tried to call them and all, but they always turn off their phones at night. That's when he called me.

Sofia: Sure. I'll drive.

Kim: Thanks. I'm kind of a hot mess right now.

They got in the car and Kim gave Sofia directions to Rick's parents as they drove.

Kim, *staring out the window in deep thought:* I know this kind of thing happens all the time to other people, I just never thought of it happening to someone I know.

In less than 10 minutes they arrived at Rick's house. It was dark.

Kim: I feel bad waking them up. But they've got to know! She lightly knocked on the door once, and before she could knock again, a light came on.

Rick's mom, Betty, came to the door and opened it.

Mrs. Lambert: Uh-oh.

She waved them in.

Kim: Mrs. Lambert, we have bad news. Rick's been in a car crash. He's at the hospital.

Mrs. Lambert: I just knew something was wrong. He's usually home early. I couldn't sleep so I finally got up…just about to check my phone when you came.

Kim: I'm so sorry.

Mrs. Lambert: Is he…alive?

Kim: Yes, but he needs surgery. We thought you would want to know.

Mrs. Lambert: Yes, of course. Thank you, dear. How bad is he?

Kim: We don't know yet.

Mrs. Lambert: Let me get Jim up. He's snoring upstairs. Nothing keeps him awake.

In a few minutes, Mr. and Mrs. Lambert came downstairs dressed and ready to go.

Kim: I'm sorry, this is Sofia. She works with me at the hospital.

Mrs. Lambert: Are you *the* Sofia who's teaching Rick about money?

Sofia: Yes, ma'am.

Mrs. Lambert: Thank you. He talks about you all the time. He wouldn't listen to us…he had to hear it from somebody else.

Sofia: We might all be that way a little bit.

Mrs. Lambert: Probably so.

Mr. Lambert, *shooing the ladies toward the driveway:* Well, let's go see what's going on.

They arrived at the ER, and upon presenting health insurance information for Rick, Mr. and Mrs. Lambert were ushered back to a surgical waiting room. Kim and Sofia followed.

They got better acquainted and chatted about all kinds of things to pass the time. Then there was lull in the conversation.

Mr. Lambert, *who had been quiet, turned to Sofia:* So, what's the next topic on your teaching agenda?

Sofia, *chuckling:* Risk.

Mr. Lambert, *with a twinkle in his eye:* Too late.

They all laughed together for the first time.

Kim: Mr. and Mrs. Lambert, I saw you give them a card to scan. Is Rick still on your insurance?

Mrs. Lambert: Yes, thank goodness. And he's on our car insurance, too. I don't know which insurance will pay for all this. Hopefully, one of them will.

Kim: Why would car insurance pay for this?

Mrs. Lambert: That's one of the things car insurance pays for, depending on your coverage and the circumstances.

Kim: Oh. That's good to know.

Sofia: We hope we never need insurance, but it sure does help when we do.

Mr. Lambert: Isn't that the truth. We just got our car back from the shop. Someone backed into us in a parking lot, but it was covered.

After another two hours in the waiting room, Mr. Lambert got up to leave.

Mrs. Lambert: You going to the bathroom *again*?

Mr. Lambert: No, I'm going to find something to eat. Anyone else want anything?

Kim shook her head.

Sofia: I could go for a brownie, but you probably won't find one here. I've checked.

Mrs. Lambert: Now that you mention it, I'm getting hungry, too.

Just then, Rick's surgeon stepped into the waiting room. They were the only ones there at that time. As he entered, they all stood up.

Sofia: Hi, Dr. Long. I was hoping Rick would get you.

Dr. Long, *smiling at the compliment:* Hi Sofia.

Sofia: These are Rick's parents.

He reached out and shook their hands.

Sofia: And this is Kim, Rick's girl, uh…a friend of the family.

Dr. Long shook her hand, then motioned for them to all sit back down.

Dr. Long: Well, Rick is a strong young man. He came through the surgery very well.

Mrs. Lambert: Is he okay?

Dr. Long: Yes. He was hit very hard. He had a collapsed lung, some internal bleeding, and his left upper arm was shattered into several pieces. That's part of why the surgery took so long. But we have him back together again.

There was a collective sigh.

Dr. Long: Rick is very lucky. It could have been much worse. The thing we will need to watch for is more internal bleeding. Our ribs are designed like shock absorbers to protect our internal organs, but they can only handle so much tension before they break. In his case, when the rib broke it caused some bruising and bleeding to his lung. We will want to follow up with another MRI within a couple days to make sure that the bleeding has stopped.

Mrs. Lambert: Thank you, doctor.

Mr. Lambert: I don't know how you do this kind of stuff.

Dr. Long: Well, I used to watch my mother sew clothes for my G.I. Joe doll. Then I went into the military and learned how to sew up real G.I. Joes.

Sofia: Dr. Long is one of the best we have.

Dr. Long: Look who's talking. Everyone wants Sofia in their department.

Sofia: Aww, that's nice of you to say that.

Dr. Long: I wouldn't say it if it wasn't true.

Sofia: Thank you.

Legacy

part three

After stopping at the vending machines and 36 more minutes of snacking and waiting, they were brought into the recovery area where they huddled around Rick's bed. He was awake, but groggy.

Rick, *hearing them shuffle up to his bed:* Well, my experiment worked.

Mrs. Lambert: What experiment?

Rick, *smiling weakly:* Wanted to see who would show up if I was on my death bed.

Each woman had her own version of a gasp.

Mr. Lambert, *without missing a beat:* Almost didn't make it. There was an old rerun on TV I wanted to see for the 17th time.

They all laughed.

Rick, *chuckling:* Fair enough.

Mrs. Lambert: Dr. Long says you were lucky. This could have turned out much worse.

Rick: You mean I could be in a morgue instead of a hospital?

Mrs. Lambert: Oh, Rick. Don't talk that way.

Rick: Isn't that what you meant?

Kim: It's good to have you back.

Rick, *looking at Kim:* I'm a little surprised you're here.

Kim, *meaningfully reaching for his hand:* I'm back too.

Sofia: How are you feeling?

Rick: Ask me when the pain killers wear off.

Mr. Lambert: Whose car were you in?

Rick: Kurt's. He was driving. Have you seen him?

Kim: No, he's the one that called me, but we haven't seen him.

Sofia, *turning to go:* I'll see what I can find out.

Rick: Don't go yet.

Sofia: Okay.

Rick: You talked about God saying, "Welcome home" and "well done."

Sofia: Yes.

Rick: Ever since, I've been curious what it would take to get him to say that to me.

Sofia: Hmm.

Rick, *waving his hand across the room:* For some reason it seems a little more relevant now.

Kim: Ya think?

Mrs. Lambert: Do you want us to leave so you folks can talk?

Rick: No, stay here. Before this happened, you guys were closer to death than I was.

Mrs. Lambert: Thanks for the reminder.

Mr. Lambert: He's right. We throw the dice every day.

Mrs. Lambert, *to Sofia:* I saw a show about near-death experiences recently. You think there's anything to that?

Sofia: I don't know, but I know everyone has a death experience.

Mr. Lambert: Nobody gets out alive.

Mrs. Lambert: What do you think happens after we die? We don't go to church, and we don't really talk about this kind of stuff.

Sofia: Well, I can tell you what I understand. You can decide where to go from there.

Mr. Lambert: You mean heaven or hell?

Sofia, *smiling:* I didn't mean it that way, but I guess you have a point. The Bible says God made us to have a forever relationship with him…maybe like good parents hope to have a lifelong relationship with their kids.

Mr. Lambert: As long as it's not a lifelong relationship of them living in my basement.

Mrs. Lambert, *hitting him on the arm:* Jim, stop goofing off. This is serious.

Sofia: God is the source of life and everything good in the world. The problem is that we keep moving away from him toward harmful choices.

Rick: Man, that explains so much!

Kim: Like what?

Rick: Just look at the news. So much of it is about bad things that happen when people make bad choices.

Kim: Wow, I never thought of it that way before.

Sofia: It's true. Think of all the pain and heartache we cause each other.

Mrs. Lambert: That *is* true.

Sofia: Now, how do you feel when your kids are fighting?

Mrs. Lambert: I hate it.

Sofia: And did you ever have to discipline your kids to get them to behave?

Mrs. Lambert, *looking at Rick, smiling but scolding:* Of course. Quite a few times.

Mr. Lambert: It started improving when we threatened to sell them to the neighbors as slaves.

Mrs. Lambert: Jim, that's not funny. People really do sell kids!

Sofia: People do sell kids, beat them, and starve them. How do you think God feels when he sees people doing things like that to his children?

Mr. Lambert, *suddenly serious:* Angry. I'm a jokester, as you may have noticed. But if you mess with my people, nobody's laughing anymore.

Sofia: God is a good father who cares about every one of his kids. And he's a good judge who doesn't ignore injustice.

Rick: So why are so many bad people getting away with so many bad things?

Sofia: Nobody's getting away with anything. Everything we do and every word we say is recorded. And we will all be held accountable for the things we do in this life.

Kim: Oh my. That's a scary thought.

Sofia: Well, it's scary for criminals but comforting for victims.

Rick: What if you're neither one?

Sofia: What do you mean?

Rick: I don't feel like a criminal or a victim.

Sofia: Yeah…hmm…God made us to love him, and we show this by *worshiping* him and by showing respect to others instead of being proud. We show it by *serving* people around us instead of being selfish. And we show it by *obeying* him and those in authority instead of being stubborn. Rick, would you say you have consistently done these things your whole life?

Rick: Well, my parents are here, so I would have to say most of my life I have not done *any* of those things very well.

Sofia: Nobody does. That's the problem. Our pride, selfishness, and stubbornness cause us to reject God as our rightful king, to turn away from him and his ways, and to set ourselves up as king instead.

Mrs. Lambert: When you say it that way, it sounds serious.

Sofia: It is. We are all guilty of high treason.

Kim: I don't mean to sound disrespectful, but so what? Why can't I just live my own life the way I want to?

Sofia: Okay, let's look at it from a practical view. Where does it take us when we walk away from the Giver of Life and his good way of living?

Everyone paused without an answer.

Sofia: We make bad choices that lead to harmful habits that lead to death. Some people move slowly away, others are racing away, but everyone is naturally moving away. Life becomes darker and more hopeless the further away from God we move. So, are we really better off without him?

Kim: I kinda see your point.

Rick: Sofia has this great ability to cheer people up.

They all laugh.

Sofia: That's the bad news. But there's good news, too. Even though we have committed high treason against our rightful king, and deserve to be banished from his kingdom, he has built a loophole in his own law so that we can be forgiven for our crimes.

Mr. Lambert: Why would he do that?

Sofia: Because he loves us and wants to restore our relationship with him.

Mr. Lambert: It's a good thing he's God and not me. I don't think I would give people a second chance.

Sofia: Oh, we need more than a second chance.

Mr. Lambert: Why?

Sofia: Have you ever lied to anyone?

Mr. Lambert: Yeah.

Sofia: More than once?

Mr. Lambert: Uh, yeah.

Sofia: Have you ever hated anyone, or stolen anything, or used God's name recklessly?

Mr. Lambert: All the above.

Sofia: How many times in your life would you guess you have broken the Ten Commandments?

Mr. Lambert: Couldn't begin to count.

Sofia: So, you don't just need a *second* chance, do you?

Mr. Lambert: Hmm. I guess not.

Sofia: In other words, we haven't just committed high treason once. We have done it over and over and over. If God wanted to prosecute us, it would be a very long list of crimes and a very long sentence.

Mr. Lambert: I thought this was the *good* news.

Sofia: It's good news because the bad news is *really* bad.

Rick: What's the loophole?

Sofia: Well, does a good judge just let criminals off as if nothing ever happened?

Mr. Lambert: Not if they care about justice.

Sofia: We are all on trial, and we are found guilty, and we have received our sentence...and then the judge's son walks into the courtroom and says, "Father, I'll take their punishment for them."

Rick: You think that's going to happen someday?

Sofia: Already did. That's why Jesus came to earth as both God and man. He lived a perfect life and offered himself as a perfect sacrifice. That's something only God could do. Then he died on a Roman cross to take the punishment we deserved. That's something only a man could do.

Rick: Why would he take our punishment if he was innocent?

Sofia: That's a great question.

Just then, a nurse came up to Rick's bed to check his vital signs. She told them things looked good, and Rick would be moving to a regular room for another day or two for observation and recovery. Because of the interruption, their conversation would have to continue another day.

Legacy

part four

Kim found Sofia at one of the picnic tables.

Kim: Mind if I join you?

Sofia, *motioning for her to sit:* Hey, Kim. How are you holding up?

Kim: Okay. Rick's doing really well.

Sofia: That's great…but you look troubled.

Kim: I can't stop thinking about our conversation in the recovery room.

Sofia: I guess we went pretty deep, didn't we?

Kim: You could say that.

Sofia: What stands out to you?

Kim: I don't usually think very far ahead, as you've probably noticed.

Sofia: I don't think you're alone…it's pretty common.

Kim: Well, you and Papa got me thinking ahead with my money.

Sofia: Good.

Kim: But then you got me thinking ahead about the afterlife.

Sofia: And?

Kim: I'm not ready. That phrase just keeps rolling through my mind, back and forth, over and over. I'm not ready. I know I need to do something about it, but I don't know what.

Sofia: We never finished our conversation, did we?

Kim: You said there was good news, but I didn't hear anything good.

Sofia: Sorry about that. Where did we leave off? What do you remember?

Kim: We are all guilty of high treason and about to be sentenced.

Sofia: Right. So, we are all facing the death penalty for high treason and many other crimes against God, when Jesus comes to take our place.

Kim: What does that mean?

Sofia: Why do you think we have Good Friday and Easter on the calendar?

Kim: I never really knew.

Sofia: Well, Good Friday commemorates Jesus dying on the cross to take our punishment, so we can be set free.

Kim: That doesn't seem fair.

Sofia: It's not fair. It's his mercy toward us. And Easter celebrates the fact that he rose from the dead.

Kim: Like for real?

Sofia: One of the best-documented events in history.

Kim: Whoa. What, everyone gets off just like that?

Sofia: It is a gift, but we have to accept it.

Kim: What do you mean?

Sofia: Some people don't see any need for Jesus because they don't think they are guilty of anything.

Kim: Oh, I know I've been a self-centered snot. When you were describing the run-my-own-life-treason thing, I was with you.

Sofia: And some people know they are bad, but they think they can just turn themselves around and try to be better.

Kim: How does that take care of anything in the past?

Sofia: It doesn't, but they think if they just try harder maybe they can be good enough for God.

Kim: That's not me. I need help.

Sofia: Then turn to God for help.

Kim: It's that easy?

Sofia: I didn't say it was easy. But it is that simple. When you walk away from your old life and come to Jesus for a new life, he forgives all the bad you've done and gives you a new start.

Kim: What do I do?

Sofia: Just talk to him.

Kim: Like he's listening right now?

Sofia: He is listening to you, and watching you, all the time, so nothing you say is going to surprise him. Just tell him where you've been and what you've done. Tell him you want to start following him from now on.

Kim: Could I do that here?

Sofia: You sure can.

Kim, *weeping:* Jesus, I'm a hot mess.

I have been such a proud and selfish person.

You made me but I've wanted nothing to do with you.

I've gone behind your back and committed high treason.

Sobbing: I've basically told myself I would do a better job of running my life than you.

That's just not true.

I need your help.

I need you in my life.

Sniffling: Would you forgive me?

Would you take over and lead me from now on?

I guess that's all.

Kim wiped the tears from her eyes and looked at Sofia.

Kim, *sighing:* Wow, I feel like a huge weight has been lifted off my shoulders.

Sofia reached out to hug Kim, and they cried together.

Epilogue

Kim and Rick started dating again.

After a few months, he asked her to dress up for one of their dates and he took her to an elegant restaurant. She appreciated doing something special for a change.

After dinner, the waiter announced that dessert was on the way. Kim was confused, since they had not ordered dessert. Next thing she knew, the waiter brought a vase with a dozen deep red roses. She was admiring them when she noticed a gold band around one of the stems. Before she could say anything, Rick dropped to one knee beside her and proposed. When she said, "Yes," he slipped the band off the rose and turning it around, she could see there was a diamond on it. As he slipped it on her finger, the crowd around them burst into applause. She started to cry and gave Rick a big hug.

They were married the next summer.

Rick's left arm was never the same after the accident. It was not as strong, or completely without pain, but that didn't stop them from enjoying a good marriage and raising three great kids: Joshua, Jessica, and Jimmy (named after Mr. Lambert).

They decided to follow Sofia's shortcuts for building wealth and avoiding hazards. Kim kept her nursing job, and Rick started a collection business.

They also started investing in real estate, which took up many of their evening and weekend hours. But it also gave them opportunities to learn and teach their kids many practical skills: framing, plumbing, painting, etc.

Rick's business kept growing, as Sofia predicted, but he and Kim were both able to keep part-time hours to make more room for real estate and family activities. They also put money into Kim's 401k at work and into a Roth IRA for Rick each year.

Within 18 years, they had about $6,000 monthly income from 10 rental units. They could have retired from this; however, they decided to wait a couple more years until they had the units paid off. Once complete, their rental income jumped to just under $10,000 per month. They used this extra income to add to their Roth IRA and help Joshua with college. He studied business and accounting.

Neither Jessica nor Jimmy went to college. Jessica had almost completely taken over Rick's collection business. She loved finding deals and cataloguing, organizing, and presenting their merchandise. She also loved working with customers. She was planning to buy Rick out of his collection business and keep growing it.

Jimmy loved working with his hands. He got a builder's license as soon as he turned 18 and started a construction business.

Kim grew close to God over the years, and this not only made her a nicer person, but she was also full of joy and peace. Rick wanted what she had, but he didn't want to turn over control of his life to anyone else, not even God. They kept talking with Sofia about money principles and God and became very close friends.

Rick eventually turned his life over to God and experienced the same freedom Kim had, and together they avoided the biggest hazard of all by going into retirement spiritually prepared.

Index of Shortcuts and Hazards

Shortcuts

- Build up ways to replace your income – Page 10
- Income as Lever #1 – Page 11
- Spending as Lever #2 – Page 11
- Appreciating assets as Lever #3 – Page 12
- Start with the walruses, not the mice – Page 21
- Paths to become a millionaire – Page 28
- Semi-retiring and/or renting out space – Page 33
- Get an annuity – Page 34
- Pay taxes on the seed instead of the harvest – Page 40
- HSAs and QCDs – Page 41
- Roth conversions – Page 43
- Life insurance – Page 44

Hazards

- Borrowing money as a negative Lever – Page 14
- Borrowing for depreciating assets – Page 16
- Sequence of return risk – Page 25
- Don't put all your eggs in one basket – Page 35
- The ticking tax bomb – Page 38

7 Key Areas for a Successful Retirement

1. **Legal:** Complete estate planning documents so that wishes are carried out and children still enjoy holidays together.
2. **Tax:** Develop tax-efficient strategies for leaving the IRS out of retirement and inheritance as much as possible
3. **Investment:** Build an investment plan aligned around family goals, concerns, and objectives for liquidity, safety, income, growth, and protection/leverage.
4. **Income:** Strategize how to optimize Social Security, pensions, investments, etc., to build a lifetime income stream.
5. **Risk:** Review insurance needs for home, auto, life, disability, liability, and identity theft.
6. **Health:** Review options to cover health benefits and long-term care needs.
7. **Legacy:** Set up a plan for making memories, making an impact, and making final arrangements.

Generation Series

Experience the Generation Series through four business parables, encountering interesting characters who reveal practical insights about work, money, life dreams, love, and people. But be careful; The trajectory of your life might change in the process.

Book 1 – **Kids Work**

The Benefits They Receive When Kids Work. Meet James, who starts out torn between a gang and the law and his neighbor, Ron Powers. Will he go to the juvenile center? Will he work with Ron? How will his decisions affect the direction of his life? This fast-moving story illustrates how enabling kids to work brings many benefits and prepares them for the real world.

Book 2 – **Dream House**

Dream House Debt Free 8-12 Years From Now. Eavesdrop as Ron Powers teaches his niece, Sofia, how she can acquire her dream house and pay it off in eight to 12 years. They bond over time as he shares many practical tips anyone could use to improve personal finances, regardless of age or housing situation.

Book 3 – **Retire Successfully**

Retire Successfully by Following Shortcuts and Avoiding Hazards. We got to know Sofia in Dream House. One of her workmates asks her how to prepare for a successful retirement and she is happy to share her secrets. Follow her example and you could be ready for your own successful retirement adventure.

Book 4 – **Legacy Living**

Be Rich Through Legacy Living. Join Jackie Powers, Ron's wife, as she introduces her cousin Lydia to some unforgettable people who each impact her deeply. She will never be the same… and you might not either.

Connect with the Author

Would you like to connect with the author? Please feel free to reach out at:
info@famfocfinancial.com.

About Family Focused Financial

Family Focused Financial specializes in retirement planning and services from a biblical mindset. Securities and Advisory Services are offered through ***Harbour Investments, Inc.*** Member FINRA/SIPC.

FAMILY FOCUSED
FINANCIAL

Scan Here!

Phone: 269-208-4237
Website: www.famfocfinancial.com
Email: Info@famfocfinancial.com

Made in the USA
Monee, IL
04 November 2026

67379946R00046